I Am
THE
Woman
AT THE
Well

Christina Jerabek

ISBN 979-8-89345-052-1 (paperback)
ISBN 979-8-89345-053-8 (digital)

Christian Faith Publishing
832 Park Avenue
Meadville, PA 16335
www.christianfaithpublishing.com

Printed in the United States of America

It has taken me seven years to write this book. I used to think it was because I didn't want people who were not saved to get a bad name from reading this book, afraid of what people may think, but it was because I was afraid of healing. I have been used to pain my whole life, and I am scared to be healed because all I know is pain. Another word for this is trauma. I said to God, without realizing it, "You can come close, but not too close. You can see this part of my heart, but not that part." One particular sin that I committed took me ten years to heal from, which you will find out when reading this book. I'm not afraid to be judged by people. True believers will understand. And as for the sinners, some will see what God can do, even for them, especially with someone like me. Here is my testimony.

Therefore I tell you, her sins, which are
many, are forgiven—for she loved much.
But he who is forgiven little, loves little.
—Luke 7:47

In the Beginning

I was three years old, and my mother and I were holding on to each other, screaming as a man punched his hand through the window of the door, trying to come inside. Then we visited this man at the hospital because he was my mom's boyfriend at the time. This is my first memory. (Later in life, I confirmed this with the man himself when I reached out to him when I was seventeen).

Let me give you some background on my family. My mother was clubfooted. She had about twenty-three surgeries on her legs. She also had multiple abortions (I was supposed to be one as well), and she was also insecure, looking for love in all the wrong places, with boyfriend after boyfriend yielding the same result: abandoned and abused.

My dad did not want responsibility. He was a very selfish man, ruled by drugs. He used my mother as well. When she got "old" (not talking about age), he went and got another woman. There was no commitment in his life.

Now the setting of my life. My parents were never married, and they fought all the time. Sadly, this had long-term effects on me because I was forced to choose between my parents, over and over again. My mom's side of the family hated my dad's side of the family and vice versa.

Thus building me up to have very low self-esteem. I would watch my mom be treated poorly by men, emotionally and physically. With my father, I would watch him have sex with my stepmom, and she would treat me poorly.

Over and over again, things had happened in my great-grandmother's care on my dad's side. A couple of times, I had to get my stomach pumped from ingesting her heart medications.

Eventually she was no longer allowed to see me because she was found guilty of molesting me.

Shortly after, when I was four years old, my mom died during childbirth. A doctor cut into her the wrong way, and she hemorrhaged to death. I remember being outside of the hospital that day, waiting for my "new" baby brother.

An investigator came to the hospital because, apparently, my mom had said something to the nurse, and an investigation was opened up after she died. I will never know what truly had gone on or what was said. I am only relaying what I was told by my aunt on this portion.

DCF has been in my life many times due to the war between my parents. After my mom died, I was placed with my aunt T for a time while my dad could show DCF that he could be a good father.

In the care of my aunt T, a boy took my innocence away when we were on his porch. I will never forget the blood running down my legs as I was screaming to try and find my aunts. But unfortunately, I found no comfort from them. They were upset at me during that time and to this day deny what happened. In a way, I can understand, though. If I were worldly, I would deny it too because I would not want to be accountable for that or have that on my conscience.

When the day came, shortly after, for my dad to get me back, he picked me up from my aunt's house. I was so happy. I was glad to have my daddy back. When my dad, stepmom, and I were in the car driving to his house, all I kept hearing was my stepmom saying such horrible things about me: "She doesn't look like you." "She's from a different man." "Her mom…," etc., etc.

As I'm hearing these lies, I'm crying at this point. I looked behind me to see if a car was behind us so I could open the door and jump out and have it run me over. I put my hand on the door to open it, and as I'm about to pull it open, I hear a voice in my head.

"Don't do it."

I respond with, "Why not?"

"Don't," the voice said.

So I listened to the voice and continued to cry all the way to my "new" home.

(In 2021, my adopted mother showed me documents from DCF paperwork from that time, and it showed one of my suicidal attempts and molestation from when I was three and four. My rape was never documented because it was never reported.)

Please know that by this time, I am a very sexualized child. I would play sexually with other children after my rape. I was molested over and over by both male and female grown-ups. I would also play sexually with my cousins. I haven't documented *every sexual event* here because there is no need.

My "New Home"

By now in my life, I'm four years old, going on five. I have had a lot of hurt and insecurity. Sadly, many kids are going through this. I was just hearing the other day how suicide is at its highest, especially with young girls. I can't give an answer to those who ask me, "Why does God allow these things to happen?" I know for me, though, I can say that it's because He wants me to see what sin does to not only myself but others, and that's why He says not to sin. God hates sin. Look at what sin does.

During this time, my age is between four and six years old. This way, you can understand because when reading this, it may seem like a few events, but this was my new, everyday life.

Here's the background: my father and stepmom were drug addicts. Pills, marijuana, heroin, and just about anything they could get their hands on.

They both were high all the time. They couldn't make the rent payments. We moved five times, I can remember. I was allowed to have one bologna sandwich a day. That was two pieces of bread and one bologna. I could choose when to have it. When

I would try to sneak bread at night and got caught, not only was I beaten for it, they locked me in my room unless I was in school. I remember a picture of me (school picture) smiling as I had a black eye. But the school was told that I had fallen when it was from abuse.

I went through not only physical abuse and neglect from my dad and stepmom but also verbal. I remember I got out of the shower one time, and my stepmom said to my dad, "See, I was right, she has black hair. She's not your daughter!" I cried. In all honesty, in my life, I had been beaten so much that it's words that hurt me the most, not the beatings. All I really wanted as a child was someone to love me and stay. (Isn't that all of us? Wanting to be loved.)

There was a point where I asked my dad what happened to my mom. He and my stepmom were smoking their cigarettes at the kitchen table, ashtray in the middle of the table. His response was this: "You see the ashes? Your mom was put naked in a box and into a furnace, and these are her ashes."

Then he and my stepmom started laughing hysterically, and I cried.

My dad and stepmom did not like me talking to people. I know my stepmom would get offended and upset when an adult took a liking to me. This memory I'm about to tell you next is beautiful but not. I just got to see what a real family was, even if it was only for a night. My dad and stepmom were trying to see if someone would adopt me. At this point, my stepmom had a baby, and I was a problem. A family had a trial run with me. I remember going to their house at night, listening to VeggieTales in the car for the first time. I remember the "The Bunny Song" and laughing at it. It was so funny. But the next day, we were at the table drawing, and I showed them the drawing I did. Well, I drew my dad's private part. That's not what a family wants to see. Well, that was the straw that broke the camel's back. What was beautiful though, I got to see what a family was like. And the dad drew me a picture, I believe it was a car, I don't remember exactly, and he said some loving words to me. I can't remember what they were, but I remember how he made me feel.

When I got back home though, my stepmom told me, "Can't you behave just once so someone can love you?"

She would tell me stuff like that all the time. In the court papers, I have read how she would tell me I was a bad girl and that's why no one loved me. I also had told DCF that I was afraid that my stepmom would kill me. I had also gone into a mental hospital because I tried to commit suicide again.

One of my last memories during this time, I remember the day very well. I was getting ready for school, and I asked my stepmom where my dad was because I wanted to give him a kiss. She said to give him a kiss when I got home. I went to school that day, and I had told the teacher that my dad had molested me. Now I don't know why I said that. But after school was out, I was waiting for my dad with high hopes because I wanted to give him a kiss, and a lady came up to me and asked me if I was Chyna Pike (my birth name). I told her yes, and she responded with her name and how she was from the Department of Children and Families. I remember we drove to Walmart right before the foster home, and she told me the government had given me two hundred dollars to spend to get something since I was going to a new home. Literally, I had been thrown around so much at this point, I wasn't even able to get attached to people. (The court papers I read did state that my dad said that he no longer wanted me and to put me in a foster home.)

So we went to Walmart, and I had so much fun. I bought two tank top shirts that had a smiley face on them. That's all I remember, shopping-wise. When we got to the foster home, I had a bed. I was sleeping on the floor in my dad's house because they didn't want to buy a bed for me. On top of my bed though was this bear. It was a Christmas bear, had the year on it, and when you press its hand, it would sing. This was around Christmastime.

I loved that bear, and it made me feel special. The other thing that made me happy was that there were other children there that I could talk to. I had a speech impediment, and people could not understand me. That night, I remember the lady saying that it was time for bed, but we pray first. So I prayed at the side of my bed for the first time in my life. This also meant I had to go to another school. Every time I moved with my dad and stepmom, that also meant that I went to a new school as well. There are a couple of fond memories I had here. Sadly though, I also was molested by a teenage boy in the home. It was coed so both boys and girls were in the same home.

Not too long after, my great-grandmother got me from the foster program, the same great-grandmother who had molested me. Now I want to point something out. When my mom died, she had my baby brother London. One of my aunts chose to adopt them and not me. My great-grandmother was found to have molested me. How they determined that, which I remember, I was in a room, in front of a mirror, and I was drawing and masturbating. This was when I was four years old. What I had drawn was a picture of my grandmother touching my private area. The court papers ended up saying that she was no longer allowed to see me. All I know is that she chose to take me when no one else would. I admire my great-grandmother. She did what so many grandparents and great-grandparents are doing today. Taking on all responsibility that they shouldn't have to, raising their grandkids.

I remember the day the DCF lady drove to see my grandmother. I remember the great joy I had when I saw her. Not having my family to then having my family. I was about seven years old. From about seven years old to ten years old, I lived with my grandma. Some of my most cherished memories are with my great-grandmother. And during this time, I was molested by a woman in our community pool. I would also watch stripper shows. I grew up watching shows like this because this is what my dad would watch. I wanted to be a stripper when I grew up.

One time I got in my grandma's lingerie, pantyhose, and high heels and posed by my grandmother's car so I could have a man stop for me. I was only seven years old. This was how corrupt my mind was; I did not know that what I was doing was not only wrong but not normal. I did a lot of sexual activity with adults, kids, and even my birth cousins. I'd constantly have night terrors. I'd wake up screaming and punching. I was very brokenhearted.

In this chapter, I'm going to tell you about all the wonderful memories I had with my great-grandmother, offering a break from pain. On a serious note: Do you see what sin does? Do you see why God hates sin—any sin, whether small or big? Sin is sin. Why does God allow bad things to happen? To show us what sin is.

Personally, I don't want to sin, nor do I want to hurt others around me. Here are memories from my heart that I want to share with you. I'd rather focus on these and not on all the garbage in my life that happened, things I didn't choose, and even the ones I did choose.

I would make boxed cakes for my great-grandmother and me. One time, one was still kind of raw, and my grandmother still ate it. Our favorite time was when it would rain, and we'd go outside on our porch to drink hot tea and play cards. My grandmother was a heavy smoker, and she is the reason I don't smoke today. Sometimes, when I came home from school, she'd say, "Chyna, look behind the door in my room." So I knew what that meant: a surprise for me. I'd run to the door and look behind it, and there would be a gift. One time, there was this "robodog"; it was a robot dog, and I loved it. She got it for me because I wanted to have a dog, and my grandmother, in her seventies, couldn't take care of one. So she thought of me when she got this present.

I've learned in life that when we have great memories, it's because that person spoke our love language, and that's why it's a memory we hold dear in our hearts. I would draw pictures for my grandma, and she would put them on her wall. I loved our Christmases. On Christmas Eve, I'd get to open one present. I was very protective of my grandma.

Now this memory I'm about to tell you is probably my most treasured. I was seven years old, watching a Christmas movie (*Precious Moments*). When I watched the little child give his gift to Jesus, I got a small shoebox and put all my most cherished toys in it. I had my eyes closed, and I prayed for the Lord to take it because I was giving it to Him. So as I was praying, I slightly opened one of my eyes, hoping to see Jesus take it.

At the end of living with my grandmother at nine, I started going to church. I wanted to, and the reason was that I met a lady named Ms. Harris. She would take me to church; little did I know, she and my grandma were looking for people to adopt me. Ms. Harris had passed out flyers to the church to adopt me. During that time with my grandmother, she would say, "Chyna, if I don't wake up, call 911."

That left me scared. I'd grab a chair and watch her sleep. She meant the world to me.

My future adoptive parents were at my grandma's trailer. I was told by them that they were looking to adopt me. So to show off, I ran as fast as I could back and forth in my grandma's trailer. I was thinking that if they could see how fast I ran, maybe they would love me. I just wanted to be loved.

I went to live with them, and a lot of my sexual behavior had calmed down. I was not used to rules. I went from complete freedom to rules. That was a good thing, even though I didn't like it. One of the first things was changing my name; that was done. My birth name was Chyna Chyanne Pike. I remember my adoptive mom giving me this book with names in it because she told me that my name needed to have a meaning and that my birth name didn't have a meaning. Of course, I was excited, but then not about getting my name changed. I wanted to change my name to Sabrina, Kristen, Serena. All were a no. At this point, I was like, I want to get this over with, so I saw the name Christina, and I showed my mom, and she said yes and gave me my middle name, Joy.

My adoptive mom, whom now I will call my mom just so you cannot get confused when I write, because when I was adopted, I became my mom's child.

My mom had a lot of work to do. I had a speech impediment. No one could really understand me. Not only did I begin homeschooling but also learning how to talk. This was torture for not only myself but my mom as well. I was behind in school and needed to catch up. I also was diagnosed with ADHD. Both my mom and I would cry because it was hard on both of us. She had sacrificed so much for me. Of course, I was a pain in the rear end. Oh, how I wish I could have appreciated my mom back then, but thank you, Lord, for not only healing but forgiveness.

I remember the day I fell in love with my mom. She was brushing my hair in the bathroom, and I smiled; I was about eleven. I heard a voice in my head that said, "She will leave you too." All of a sudden, I hardened my heart because I didn't want to get hurt again. This was the day they dedicated me into the church. Now I lived with two brothers and two sisters, and I was the second youngest child. So we were a family of seven. Now I had problems, but this started more problems.

My mom believed that because I would go and visit my grandma and come back acting rebelliously, crying, heartbroken, I needed not to see her again. So I didn't. That was my biggest heartbreak. My grandma was my everything. I can understand why my mom did it. It's hard because, being in her shoes, you want your daughter to move forward in her new life. You want your daughter to start healing from all those traumas associated with the past and also that family. What do you do? There isn't a book out there that man has written that says, "Hey, what to do with a little girl that has gone through everything imaginable that's bad, and here's the answers." My mom did the best with what she knew and going to the Lord and praying. Guess what, mistakes were made, but I know that my mom made that choice because she loved and still loves me. I will also share my last visit with my grandma as well.

The last time I visited my grandma, it was my adopted dad, my adopted little brother, and me. I remember I was looking at a picture on the wall of my two twin cousins and me. I heard a voice say to me, "Ask your grandma who the picture on the wall is."

I responded in my head with, "I don't need to, my grandma already knows."

The voice responded with, "Just ask."

So I asked my grandma who the picture on the wall was. And of course, I knew she was going to say that it was me. She stated, "That is my grand-daughter, Chyna." I responded with, "Yes, Grandma, that's me." My grandma then replied, "You're not my granddaughter, I don't know who you are." That tore my heart. I cried. And for years, that memory hurt me dearly.

From fourth to sixth grade, I was in a church program called Missionettes. It starts from first grade, I believe. There's a curriculum, and based on the amount finished, we were awarded badges, and you are crowned a certain star, the highest being an Honor Star. I knew I was able to see my grandma, and I did the best I could. My mom sent her an invitation to my ceremony. It was graduation, Wednesday night; we all got dolled up in beautiful gowns and sashes. I remember having the butterflies, getting to see my great-grandmother for the first time in a long time. As we all got on stage, I scanned the crowd to find my great-grandmother. As I'm getting crowned an Honor Star, I said to myself, *I did it all for nothing*.

That night, I was destroyed. I hid behind my smile. Not too long after that, I kept getting the same dream. The dream was that my great-grandmother had died, and I was searching for my birth mom's belongings. So I snuck onto the computer (I wasn't allowed on the Internet because I had looked up inappropriate images, females to be exact) and found my grandma's obituary. I then hated my mom. I wanted her to know my pain and to go through having to be torn away from the only one who had loved me, then taken away and never being able to see her again because she was gone. I did everything I could think of to cause her pain. I started cutting myself and tried killing myself many times, from hanging myself in my closet, taking ten of my sibling's acne pills, and trying to fume my room with Axe spray and hairspray, to many other poor decisions.

I would throw my things and cut my wrists to bleed out and my ankles, legs, and upper arms. I had a problem with bulimia. I'd done this for a few years but finally stopped eating. I was done with life; my shorts would just fall on the floor off of me. My mother told me to eat, or I'd get a feeding tube. People at church would tell me I was getting too thin. I'd tell my mom over and over again to put me back in foster care, or I will die. I'd smash windows and destroy my belongings. It was like a tornado went through the room. I kicked holes in the walls. I'd even hit myself. I needed to be punished.

My behavior was so bad that I had gotten expelled from one Christian school for cussing out the pastor. Even in middle school, I had a lot of problems. People would make fun of me because I was bisexual. I stood up for my sexuality because I saw no problem with loving who I wanted to love. In reality, even though I didn't see it, I just wanted to be loved. Even when I had a girlfriend in high school, she, too, left me. She cheated, and her saying, "Hate the game, not the player," was when I saw that even women would fail me.

You know, there's a point of view that I have not even shown here. I've only shown my side—the hurts I went through, both the pain that I did not choose for me and the pain I did choose. My brothers and sisters were afraid of me. There's so much pain; I caused so much pain in them. My parents almost got a divorce because of me. I hurt so much for my brothers and sisters (me being saved now) because I wish I could take their pain away. I wish I had never put them through the pain of my behavior. They watched me physically abuse my mom and hurt her very much, and I took so much time away that she could have spent with them but instead spent with me because I was a rebellious and angry child.

This was how bitter my heart became. My mom had gone to Israel and bought promise rings for my brothers and sisters, and for me, she got a beautiful hat and a bracelet. I asked her why she didn't get me a ring, and she responded that I wasn't ready.

Now she was right. During that time, my mindset was, *If you think that I will prove you right.* So I started sneaking over to my boyfriend's house at night and having sex. I was sixteen. Now this was during the end of me living with my parents. I had gone into a teenage house and was also molested there, but I felt accepted there because I was bisexual. When I came back home, that's when I stopped eating. I ended up having another outrage and threw part of my dresser at the window and tried getting through it to run away and started cutting myself with a glass of the window. Now I had run away before, but this time, my parents had me detained. From what I remember, the ambulance came and got me. Multiple times I had gone into the psych ward, but I had gone into the hospital first, where I was told that I was pregnant.

When the hospital told me that I was pregnant, I called my boyfriend from the hospital and told him. I was amazed that life could be growing in my stomach, so I began eating again. I no longer wanted to die. The hospital then transferred me to the mental hospital, and there they told my mom that I was pregnant. Of course, my parents were upset. When I came home, I would rest on my side and no longer want to be at war. You'd understand the situation because even my family did not know what I did next. They were constantly walking on eggshells. They then had to make a decision: I needed to marry because I was pregnant. My parents and my boyfriend's parents sat down and talked. I don't remember everything said, but all I know was I was excited to start a new life with my boyfriend and our baby. I talked to my mom recently about this. She didn't want me to marry, but God had told her to let me go.

We got married, and I thought my life would then start. I was wrong. I thought my boyfriend, now my husband, was my savior. I thought I could trust him, but I couldn't. He came to me and told me that if I didn't have an abortion, he would kick me out of the house, and I'd be homeless. I was afraid. So I went to get an abortion. I didn't want to. My mother-in-law brought me there and acted like everybody does it. So not only was there a lot of physical pain in my body, but I held the remains of my child in a tub as I aborted my child. I then told myself that I would never forgive my husband and would hurt him like he hurt me. A few days later, a woman from my church, who used to be my old Bible quiz coach, came to my front door with gifts. She was the only one who was supportive, and she came to the front door and said, "Chyna," with a smile on her face.

I broke down and told her, "You're too late," and I slowly shut the door. Ma'am, if you ever read this book, thank you for being there. I had no one, and you showed kindness to me, even when I did not deserve it.

During this time, I got to meet my brother, London. It was a day I will never forget. My husband and I drove all through the day, and at night, I saw my brother for the first time. I was sixteen. I felt a sense of hope. Like I got some of my heart back. I remember being in middle school, and our teacher asked us a question about abortion. This was when I was in seventh grade. She asked, "When is it okay to have an abortion?" And we would debate. I kept silent, just listening to people's responses. They started to agree that it was okay to have an abortion if the mother was going to die. The teacher disagreed, and the class didn't like it. That's when I spoke up. I told the class that I had experienced this, and they could understand from someone who was in that situation what the answer is. I told them that I was glad that my mom had my brother, even though she was told by the doctor that she was going to die and that I was taken away from my brother. I lost both, but for the fact that he's even alive, and if I'd never meet him, I'm glad that my mom didn't abort him. I told the class that it did hurt that I no longer had my mom, but I was glad to have a baby brother, even though I didn't know where he was.

During my marriage, I started to cut again. I started to be suicidal again. We were arguing at one point, and I grabbed a steak knife and sliced my throat because I wanted to die, but the knife didn't slice, didn't tear my skin at all. Then it came to me that I didn't want to die. So I said to myself, *I will cheat on him*, and I did. I was seventeen, and I was sleeping with a thirty-eight-year-old man. I wanted to get him back tenfold. We ended up getting divorced, and I moved in with a thirty-eight-year-old. The thirty-eight-year-old, and I worked together at Sub Shop, and everything I made went to him. I worked about sixty hours a week, and a lot of my pay was under the table. He introduced me to Xanax and other pills. I was then a functioning alcoholic. I'd wake up and would drink, then work, and alcohol would be in my drink cup. Not too long after, I walked in the door of the apartment, and he had a couple of men at the table doing cocaine. They were drug dealers from Miami, and he told me to take my clothes off and dance for them. I told him no, and he told me that if I didn't entertain them, then he would, and he did. He'd get the dog training collar, it's a heavy metal leash, and he whipped me with it over and over and over again. I felt the pain on my body and my head (which I have star prints from the metal prongs on my head to this day and knuckle prints). I remember them laughing. This happened over and over again.

I had gone to work, and a customer asked me who was beating me. I looked at the thirty-eight-year-old man and saw him make a fist underneath the cutting board. I responded to him that I liked having hot sex, and he said to me, "You may fool other people, but you can't fool me." I wanted to be saved. I was tired and afraid. I couldn't get out. I was underweight again and at the point where I needed surgery on my throat. I had to have my tonsils removed and had a cyst behind them. I couldn't breathe. All I did was drink, mostly vodka, overdose on pills, and not eat. The doctor did my surgery for free. I was seventeen, had no money, and I was told that if I didn't have surgery, I wouldn't have much time.

After I had surgery, I went back to the thirty-eight-year-old's house. I had a new boyfriend, but I had to hide it because I didn't want him killed. That night, I went back to my apartment, and this guy was drunk, again. He, too, was a functioning alcoholic, but this time, he told me it was time to do cocaine. I told him no, and I ran out of that place as fast as I could because I didn't want to get beaten again. I called my boyfriend, and he took me to his home. As for the thirty-eight-year-old, he threw my stuff out and had me fired from my job. I don't know what was said, but I was happy that I was away from him. I'd wake up screaming because I thought he had come to kill me. So my boyfriend introduced me to marijuana. At this point, I was still doing pills, but marijuana helped me sleep.

I contacted my mom. I don't remember this portion of my life; I was a drug addict. I remember vividly things here and there. I remember telling her that I was pregnant, and she said that I needed to marry. I was turning eighteen at this time. My boyfriend and I did marry. I wanted her in my life. He was twenty-seven at the time. Again, I thought he was my savior. There is beauty in this relationship. I tried to live for God. I tried to live by the commandments, which I epically failed at. I even dedicated our son, Micah, to the Lord. I was even baptized. But I left the church right after the children's pastor called my son a sin baby because he was conceived when my husband and I were dating and not married. My cousin would come over with church friends, and I remember telling them, "My home is your home, but don't talk to me about Jesus. I tried it, and it didn't work for me." My personality people loved, but when I was angry, people were scared. I've been called Angelic Demon by many people, and these people didn't even know each other. People would say I was the nicest person they ever met but also the scariest person.

Shortly after having my son, I began to treat my second husband poorly. One time, he was sleeping with our baby on him, and the baby had fallen off and got stuck between a side table and the bed. I told him how stupid he was, etc. I didn't trust him with our son. I viewed him as the enemy. I worshipped my son. (You know, looking back, I thought about the words I would have said and about how scared he was too.) I avoided intimacy with my husband, and our marriage fell apart. He then was getting his needs met by another woman. So I was going to get him back.

I went online, met another man, and had relations with him. I wasn't ashamed. I didn't hide my sins; I let them all out. I knew the verse, "Make sure your sins will find you out." My thought was, *I'm an adult, and if I want to sin, I don't need to hide it.* That is one of the most dangerous places for your heart to be at, to no longer care about hurting anyone and that you enjoy it.

My separation and divorce were horrible, consequences to this day that are in my life because of my sin. When people start understanding what sin does, they're not going to want to sin anymore. Sin has hurt me and everyone around me. You see it here in this book what sin does and the domino effect it has.

When I look back, I am ashamed. Because of the hurt I was experiencing during my separation from my husband, I made so many stupid mistakes. I started to do cocaine, leaving my son with his father because I just didn't care about being a mom anymore. I still loved my son, but I didn't know how to heal. So I went back to what I knew that brought comfort, and that was drugs, but this time, I went to a higher high. And I was prostituting my body to get these drugs. Sometimes I didn't even get the drugs because I was lied to, but it was too late at that point. The deed had been done, and no transaction was gained from it.

My husband's side of the family did not like me from the beginning, so they started making false DCF complaints toward me, to where they were saying that I was raping my one-year-old son. I won't get into detail about what they stated, but it's disgusting. Of course, there was an open investigation with no findings, but that sent me to where I needed to be high all the time. I had no idea that I had PTSD at this time. I just couldn't believe they would stoop that low to say that about me during that time. I didn't want to relive what I had gone through, and with this comment, I was reliving the trauma that I was running away from.

For the man I met online, I went up to Connecticut to meet him. Was up there for a week and fornicated. And when I came back to Florida, he shortly followed. When he came down, I decided to live in the woods with him. We had a tent in the woods. We would take showers in the woods with gallons of water. Sometimes I would take a shower at Lakes Park until a worker who worked there said that if I showed up again, they would get a no-trespassing order against me. I tried getting my son back. I'd walk a total of four hours, round trip for a two-hour shift. I hadn't worked since I was pregnant with my son, I was a stay-at-home mom. So I worked at Taco Bell. I ended up sending my boyfriend, T, back to Connecticut. I was able to have a free burrito per shift, and I'd give it to my boyfriend so he wouldn't be hungry. The little money I did get from these shifts, about fifty dollars a check a week, I'd buy vodka to put in my drink at work, and I was tipsy as the cashier. I just didn't want to live anymore. I had no hope. Another coworker knew I wanted to get my son back, so he told me that his cousin could offer me a job. So I said okay. He told me his cousin was outside in a van and told me that he wanted to speak to me in the van. I thought that was a little weird, but this was one of those vans that you could fold down the back seat into a bed, and it had some seats facing it. So it was roomy. His cousin had a girlfriend, and they both talked to me. They said that the job was me taking men out on dates. Nothing more. Just old men, who lost their wives and want to have a friend.

I said I could do that. They said, "Okay, be prepared to come with us the next night, and we will take care of you."

Well, I thought it was a dream come true. I could finally get my son back. Over and over again, I tried seeing my son, and my husband was withholding him from me. I went through a lot of abuse, and an event that took place with my husband and me that I will not disclose, in case my son ever did read this book.

The next day, I got into the van; it was night-time. I was so happy to leave. Having to walk at 12:00 a.m. downtown, after work, with men harassing and following me, was a nightmare. Freedom at last. Hopes of getting my baby boy back.

Well, we came to a hotel. I was talking for a while to the girl while her boyfriend went into the hotel room. I asked her where he was going, and she said that he was freshening up. Then came the point when her phone went off, and she told me to go to the hotel room. I responded with, "Okay, are you coming?"

She said, "Yes, I will be right behind you, go ahead."

So I went into the room, and it was dark. I heard the man say, "Sit down," so I did, thinking this was weird. He came to me, grabbed my head, and told me what sexual act I was going to do to him because he now owned me. There was now no way out for me.

Afterward, his girlfriend came in, and I had to wash up so they could take pictures of me and make a profile for me. I was being sold for two hundred roses. I was then told what I needed to do. The wording I needed to say and to never be handed the cash but to have the person set it on the table because that was considered a transaction if payment was to be put in my hand. I was informed of the possibility of a police officer being a client of mine. I was now an escort.

During this time, there was another girl as well. We would travel to different hotel rooms. I was doing cocaine, pills, and marijuana. The girls loved doing this, but I didn't. I couldn't even look at myself in the mirror anymore. The fear and anxiety of not knowing who would come to my room and that I had to have sex with them. I had to compete with other women. Tons of girls from fourteen years old and higher, all around in the hotels that we were at. One point, I saw another pimp who wasn't from our group; his trunk was loaded with guns. The pimp that we had, he would ask his girlfriend to spot other vulnerable women and also prostitutes. All the money that I did get no longer was mine. I remember a few weeks into it, I prayed to God. I said, "Lord, please save me." We went to another hotel, and they would be on the phone talking to my next client. Little did I know, my next clients were two cops. The reason why I knew that was because the pimp had heard next door the same conversation his girlfriend was having and the men saying that they were watching me in the lobby of the hotel room.

The pimp and his girlfriend were in fear. They told me what was going on and told me that I could no longer associate with them and said that they were going to get me a bus ticket. I asked them to get me for Connecticut so I could be with my boyfriend. Now I wasn't allowed to communicate with the outside world at this time, I was hoping that T still loved me. They got me the bus ticket and left me a little bag of cocaine as a departing gift. That's what they said, but I wonder if it was to get me busted with it. Not sure. In the drug life, when people say they are your friends, it never turns out that way. I remember one of the stops that the Greyhound bus took, I remember saying to myself, *I am going to start anew.* So right in front of the bus driver, not realizing it, I emptied out my bag of cocaine in the trash, looked up, and see the bus driver's face jaw dropped. I still laugh at that.

When I got to Connecticut, I informed my boyfriend, T, what had happened. But instead of treating me with love, in his eyes, I was a prostitute. He treated me like I wanted to do those things. Especially when I found out a month later that I was pregnant. I remember when getting the mammogram, T had said one of the nastiest things to me, accusing me that the baby in my womb was from one of the men that I prostituted with. It did scare me, but I was going to have this baby because I regretted having the first abortion. If I had known that there was a place I could go and help out there, I wouldn't have had it. What's done is done.

During this time, I was at high risk for pre-eclampsia. We were homeless, living in the woods in below-zero-degree weather. The family didn't approve of me. Rejected again. Finally, after a few months, his parents allowed us to live with them. His sisters did not like me, and we fought like cats and dogs. I would put hair remover in her shampoo bottle, and she would do things back to me as well. I laugh now, and I have so much love for them. One day, I hope they, too, will feel the same way.

During my pregnancy, I was fighting in the courts to get my son back. I was letting the mediator know that Micah was being withheld from me when I lived in Florida, and my husband's lawyer was accusing me of abandonment due to me leaving the state. I had no idea about laws, etc., and I lost in court, on my birthday, to be exact, October 15, 2012. I left Connecticut to go to Florida for the court hearing for the divorce and showed up five minutes late. I didn't see my husband there. It wasn't until about ten minutes later that the judge asked me what I was there for. I told her the case name, and she responded with, "I've heard a lot about you." Those are the only words I can remember. The words after were very hurtful. This lawyer lied on a lot of the court documents. I had proof, but the judge didn't want anything to do with me. She let me know that she gave everything to my husband, including custody, and I was worthless. I remember walking out and crying. I got on the elevator and cried out to God, "Where are you?"

I heard Him say, "Do you remember when I asked you to ask your grandma who the picture on the wall was?"

I responded with, "Yes?" crying, and He said, "I had you ask because I wanted you to know that I was always there for you."

My birthday, the day I lost my son, was the day that I finally knew that God was real. The birth of me knowing who God was.

T and I, during the pregnancy, had some good times, but mostly bad. There was a lot of physical abuse. T even had his troubles from his past too. He was disowned by his biological father, but he did get a dad in his life whom his mother married and who received T as his own. During this time, neither I nor T did drugs. I was excited to start my life with T.

One night, we were physically fighting, and my water broke. I went to the hospital and completely forgot about the fight. He had so much joy that the baby looked like him, because it was his. That was a relief for me. I was so scared of being rejected if he wasn't his. We named him Preston Joseph B., Preston by his dad, Joseph by me, because I thought about Joseph and the coat of many colors.

The fighting didn't stop, and one night, with Preston being a couple of weeks old, T started to freak out and said that he was going to kill Preston. He started to get up, and I got up in front of the baby and told him that before he got to my son, he'd have to go through me. Preston had bad colic. At that point, I was in fear. I had messaged people on

Facebook looking for help. A lady, whom I didn't even know, opened her home to me in Florida. I talked to T and told him I was going to Florida just temporarily, and I'd be back. I told him that I was leaving all my belongings with him, so he'd know I'd come back. But I wasn't going to be back. I left my birth mom's letter to my dad and drawing, my great grandma's letters that she sent me through the mail, my birth pictures, everything that was memories. All I had left, which when he found out I wasn't going to be back, he burned them with his friends. I don't regret my decision, but it still hurt.

I had to restart again, tried looking for a job, but couldn't get hired. Became homeless again, shortly after being received in the woman's home. Her son didn't want me there anymore. I had meddled in his affairs with his mom. Had one night in a motel room, bugs everywhere. I felt like a horrible mother. I didn't know how Preston and I would make it. He was only a few months old at this point. My aunt suggested coming to live with her. I got to eventually live on my own. She was upset at me for a time because I did not appreciate her, not intentionally. I was just a selfish person. I laugh because when someone is in so much sin, they tend to be the victim in everything. Granted, a lot of bad, messed-up things happened to me, not by choice, but a lot of bad things happened to me because I did choose to make poor choices.

When I got into my first apartment, my aunt and I decorated it together. I had so much fun. We even decorated my wall with condoms, but this was in mockery of me that she did it. Now a little background about my aunt. She was the one who adopted my brother the day my mom passed. She miscarried the day my mom died. She says that she traded babies with my mom. My aunt has gone through a lot of hurt in her life. Her dad committed suicide. My aunt has many wounds. God is still, to this day, calling out to her. My aunt talked my mom into having many abortions, which my mom did. I, too, was supposed to be an abortion, but thankfully, my mom chose to have me. My son Preston looks like London, my brother, the one my aunt adopted. She took a fancy to my son. My aunt likes to be a caregiver when she chooses who it will be. It makes her feel good, to the point of being like God. My aunt is also a practicing witch. I've had to teach my kids that she isn't speaking to my birth mom or birth brother, that they were demons. (Yes, my brother has passed, I'm talking current day.)

During this time, I ended up being stupid again and went on dating sites. I was running away from pain again to another man. One night, that was it, and surprise, surprise, surprise, I'm pregnant again. My aunt told me that I needed to have an abortion. Of course, I'm pigheaded and stubborn, and I told her no. That made her furious. She was right that I was not a good mom. I can't deny that at all; I agree.

You'd think, *When has this girl had enough?* Apparently, not enough. In reality, I had no idea what life was about. I had no direction. No guidance. Well, I walked to work, and my aunt would watch my son when I was at work. One night, being about six months pregnant, I come home, and the police are in my home. I go in, and there are condoms all over the floor, and I'm shocked. All of a sudden, this police lady is yelling at me that I have punched my son in the eye. A few nights before when my aunt had picked me up from work, he had a swollen eye. My aunt said she didn't know what had happened; it just appeared. So trusting her, I went to the ER, and the doctor had him transferred to All Children's Hospital because it was actually a disease leading to the brain that would have killed him if it hadn't been caught. So, already, I had to go through the possibility of losing another son.

DCF was there, and they asked me to take a drug test, which I did, and turned positive for marijuana. My aunt was telling them that I abused my child, and she would take him to live with her. I said that what she said was a lie, and I had proof that I didn't punch my son, that it was a disease. Lo and behold, the papers I had in my drawer were gone. My aunt had set it up; that's why I had to walk home from work. So with the DCF worker, we went to the ER, and thankfully the doctor who saw my son was there. He stated the truth to the DCF worker that this was not an abuse situation, that he saw us earlier in the week, and it was a disease from the eye to the brain. Well, the DCF worker apologized to me and started crying. I asked him why he was crying, and it was because I was going to go to the facility where they have the investigators there that take the children away from the parents, and that everyone who has been investigated has had their children taken away.

That night, I couldn't sleep. It was the last time I'd see my son again. I just held him in my arms the whole night, silently crying while he slept. You see, when I was pregnant with this child, I asked God to let him look like my son, Micah, because I had a lot of hurt. I couldn't bear losing another baby. I did have a problem with connecting to my son and future children as well. I was afraid of getting too attached because of the possibility of losing them just like when Micah was taken from me. The next day, the DCF worker drove me to the place, and I was investigated. At the end of it, the lady announced that it was obviously this disease (I forgot what it was) and that there was no need for me to be there. She walked me to the elevator, and as I got on with my son, she turned to me and asked if I was disabled. I looked at her, confused, and responded with no, and she said, "I just wanted to know."

From that point, my aunt stopped talking to me. And I again became homeless. I couldn't afford the rent because I made just enough to pay for day-care. I ended up having my daughter at a place that another guy I was dating and I were renting. He wanted to marry me, but shortly, a month after my daughter was born, he left to be with another woman. I wasn't too devastated about that. There was a lot of abuse. Not only to me but also to my son and his son. At one point, he was going to beat his son, which made him feel good, and I got in the way and redirected him away from the idea. His parents came and picked him and his son up, and we parted ways. As for me, apparently rent hadn't been paid, promises were made to the owner that I had no idea about, and when the owner came to me, he asked for the rent, and I told him I didn't have it, that I thought the boyfriend had paid. The boyfriend was saving money to leave, which I found out later, and I found out that he had been doing heroin in my car on the job. It was a blessing.

Due to the pain and fear, I'd hold parties at my house for the short time I had left. Drinking and drugs. I didn't want to have to deal with the reality of being once again a failure. I was looking for another boyfriend, and I found one at my job. All the guys there would make bets on who would sleep with me first. With me, I liked the challenge. I saw that one guy didn't want me, and lo and behold, I wanted him then. It's disgusting how I thought. I was still bisexual at this time. Getting my entertainment from women at a tease club, and I didn't mind my new boyfriend joining me to watch. I always thought it would be nice if I could be a man because I always felt like a man and protective over women, but only when I wanted to. I mainly wanted them for sex.

By this time, I had moved in with my boyfriend after a few months of dating. It was the life: drugs, drinking, and video games. All I had to do was leave the kids in their room, and they could play while I had my time. I needed to change jobs at the time because I had a good way of telling people off at work when it needed to be done. I have no problem speaking, but how you do it is another thing. I was tired of working in fast food or pizza jobs. So I decided to work for a nursing home. All I could get was a housekeeping job. Now I have always had a place in my heart for the elderly. I believe it was because the person who loved me the most, from my birth family, was my great-grandma. I don't like to see people in pain. No matter my nasty behavior, when it came to the elderly, there was a love there that I can't explain. I now know what that is: Christ's love. Well, it was at the end of March 2015 that I got a job there. I had to drive almost an hour to get there. Better pay, so it was worth it, and I made sure that what I did was the best I could do. Even though I wasn't saved at the time, God's Word would still come to me because I knew verses like, "Make sure your sins will find you out." Because of that verse, I stopped hiding my sin. I knew the Word was true.

I am pregnant at this point. Well, in April, I started to clean the clients' rooms in the Alzheimer's unit. By this time, I didn't count the cost of driving all that way; I wanted a job closer to home. (I literally went from job to job; I'd last about three months and then needed a new one.) I loved looking at people's rooms to see their personalities, something more interesting than my life, and I saw this poem in this person's room. What caught my attention was this "Footprints in the Sand" only because one of my good memories with my adopted family was being given a "Footprints in the Sand" picture frame for my birthday from someone, and I have no clue what I did with it. So I read the poem:

"Footprints in the Sand"

One night I had a dream. I was walking along the beach with my Lord. Across the dark sky flashed scenes from my life, and for each scene, I noticed two sets of footprints in the sand, one belonging to me and one to the Lord.

When the last scene of my life flashed before me, I looked back at the footprints in the sand. I noticed that many times along my life's pathway, especially at the lowest and saddest moments, there was only one set of footprints.

This troubled me, and I asked the Lord about it. "Lord, You said if I followed you in life, You'd walk with me all the way. But I noticed that during the most difficult times of my life, there was only one set of footprints. I don't understand why, when I needed you the most, You would leave me."

He whispered, "My precious child, I love you and will never leave you during your times of trial and suffering, When you saw only one set of footprints, it was then that I carried you."

Reading that and the emotions I poured out, tears running down my cheeks, I finally surrendered to the Lord.

I ended up getting another job. I do believe that God led me to that nursing home for that reason, and when I got saved, it was time to move forward. I ended up getting a job at Publix. I remember the first incident when God worked on me. I saw a man and his girlfriend in my line when I was a cashier, and as I looked at this woman's chest that she was exposing, I thought, *How disgusting is that.* I'm laughing as I'm typing this because I'm like, *Girl, you did way worse things than that woman exposing her chest.* This is how beautiful the Lord is.

I heard Him say to me immediately following my comment, "You don't know what she is going through. I do." Immediately, it's like the scales fell from my eyes, and I saw that this lady was being abused by this man. I started to then pray for the woman. Now to better understand my background with women, it was this: I hated women but yet at times felt protective. The reason why I hated them was because my birth dad chose my stepmom over me. So any and every woman was a threat. I felt like

I had to compete with women to get attention from men because I didn't like abandonment, and instead of blaming it on Satan, I blamed it on women. So God was healing my heart without me even realizing it.

The next thing that happened at Publix, this lady came through my line talking about how some man shot her cow, and she is crying over it. My first thought was, *This lady is crazy, all over a dead cow.* Well, lo and behold, all of a sudden, I felt her pain, and I was weeping over her and comforting her to where she was showing me pictures of her cow. And when she left my lane, immediately the feeling went away, and I then understood what compassion was. God was having me experience emotions. I had been so numbed by pain that I didn't know how to feel anymore, and he was definitely changing me. My last big thing at Publix was this. I was having complications with my pregnancy. I was having blue lips, my skin was gray, I was puking up blood and bile, and I couldn't keep anything down. I saw a lady in the store, and I heard God tell me to ask that lady to pray for me. So I did. I said, "Ma'am, I need you to pray for me, something is not right with my pregnancy." And she did.

During this time, I saw on the news station a story about a car wreck that a lady had gotten into. As the ambulance was about to leave because the lady was dead, they heard a woman's voice say, "Save my baby." They looked around, and there was no one. But they rechecked the car, and the baby was under the seat of the car. They said that that baby was a miracle baby, and her name was Lily. When I watched that, and they said, "Lily," my baby hit my stomach from the inside, and I said, "Is this the name you want?" Why I tell you this story is because when I went into labor and had my daughter, the nurse didn't understand why she was still purple after being delivered. She noticed that my daughter's umbilical cord was wrapped around her neck, and my doctor said that my child should have died in my womb and that she was a miracle baby.

God was definitely doing the work. At this point, my boyfriend and I lost our place and moved in with his mom. We are having many struggles at this point because we are unequally yoked. I had put the gaming controller down because, after being saved, God revealed to me, while I was playing a game, how my son came in to ask me a question, he's two at this time, and I barked at him for disturbing me. I remember looking at that controller, and I said to myself, *If this is how I am when I play, I don't need to play this at all.* Seeing his face, his face of rejection, still brings tears to my eyes. That I caused that baby pain over a stupid video game.

I also was no longer doing drugs or drinking alcohol. God immediately took that away. No cravings, nothing. So we really didn't have anything in common but our daughter.

I would try to have him get into the Word, but it was rejected. We tried counseling. It couldn't work. I remember during this time, I heard God say, "Your faith is about to grow." Talk about uh-oh. I did not like hearing that. What's God going to do this time? Well, about a week later, I'm reading in Ecclesiastes, "A time for seasons, a time for change," and I ask God, "Lord, why are you having me read this today?" Well, surprise, surprise. After some nasty words exchanged between my boyfriend's mother and me, I ended up in the homeless shelter with my children. No car. No money. And I'm about to lose my job due to now not having transportation.

My boyfriend broke up with me that day, and I was devastated. Rejected again. I journaled every day during that time. I had a baby who was a couple of months old, plus my one-year-old and my two-year-old, and no family to help. I was really scared. At this point, I did have a temptation of pills come into play. A "CNA" came to the abuse shelter, and I became friends with her. I was just being used for money. I had a child support payment of eight hundred dollars come in the week after I got there. God was looking out for me. We went to this club, and of course, I don't take these places seriously. I'm that weird white chick in black dress and combat boots, doing weird white chick moves on the dance floor. Well, the lady is my ride, so where she goes, I go. Well, she went to shack up with this guy she met at the party, and I didn't know this at the time, but he had a friend, and she tells him that he can shack up with me. Well, we get to his house, and they're in the bedroom, and I'm on the couch and reject the dude's friend. So we just watch *Gilmore Girls* all night, and yes, I'm wide awake because I want to get out of there. Well, the next day, after giving her money to borrow, which I never got back, she gave me a pill. And I took it, and I was feeling a good high on my bed and slept. Of course, now the conviction of the Holy Spirit is still at play, and I realized, *What are you doing?* I immediately was shown what I'd usually do when I'm rejected—men and pills and alcohol, which I did have at the club. I no longer talked to the CNA and very quickly, she left the shelter.

I started to go to God. I was not used to praying, especially because I didn't know how to give God control because I was used to being the one in control all the time. This was the first thing I needed. I needed shoes for my son because he didn't have any. I went to Walmart to buy shoes, and a couple that was there, I didn't know them, never met them before, came up to me and said, "God laid it on our hearts to buy your son a pair of shoes." I cried. I was very thankful. My emotions, I felt defeated, dragged through the mud, a horrible mother who again failed her kids.

After that, I needed diapers and wipes, and I remember asking God for them and saying, "I know you will provide." Well, I was given a whole box of packages of wipes and a couple of boxes of diapers. My faith did start to grow. Now I walked everywhere with my kids. I'd walked to this church down the street, which was an awesome church. I loved the pastor there, and I truly felt loved. I was given a Bible there, which I still have to this day. That church was truly God's church. I kept to myself being homeless; I didn't tell people because I didn't want people to feel bad for me. I didn't want any attention. Well, the pastor had found out from this other girl who also came with me a couple of times to church. I remember how he seemed, in a way, disappointed that I didn't tell him that my kids and I were homeless. Well, that Christmas, the church gave us a good Christmas, and when the time came that I got my own apartment, they even made by hand beds for my children.

While I was in the homeless shelter, God was doing work, not only building my faith but also reconciling a relationship that I had destroyed. A relationship that, secretly deep down, I wanted because I truly did love this woman. It was my adopted mom. I ended up giving her a call and let her know what was happening in my life, and we started talking on the phone. It literally had been ten years, ten years of silence. For all the praying parents out there for their prodigal children, keep praying, don't give up. God was healing me.

During my time in the homeless shelter, I had a person pay to fix my teeth's cavities, got a good job and my own car, an apartment, and I got out of a few thousand dollars in debt I had as well. I was in the homeless shelter for about six months, and I learned a lot about God, but more so about healing.

I took a trip to meet my mom. It was a four-hour drive to see her. During this time, I not only got back with my daughter's father but also was on a Christian chat site. Stay tuned…

When I saw my mom for the first time in ten years, not everyone would be able to grasp the feeling I was trying to explain. But one day, everyone who's a follower of Christ will see their saved loved ones who have gone to be with the Lord. My mother and I talked for a good while and forgave each other. I got to see my sisters and one of my brothers. They were all different. And we talked about God, which I loved. Back home, where I was, I didn't have that. The pastor of the church had to retire because he had dementia. I didn't want to leave. My mom was so beautiful, and she still is. You know, I remember telling my mom, "Mom, I don't need a man, I'm happy with God." Lo and behold, Satan comes to destroy. At this time, I never realized how important the church is; I wasn't going, and the "fellowship" that I was getting online wasn't fellowship.

This is how husband number 3 came about.

While I was on this Christian chat site, I fell in love head over heels for a guy named J. He was a teacher, teaching the Bible, and had some attitude problems. He would debate till he was blue in the face. That was what intrigued me so much. I had grown up in middle and high school in a program that quizzed in the Word, to where in high school, instead of just memorizing questions and answers from the Word, you would then memorize a whole book from the Bible that year and compete in your state. I loved to debate, and I loved knowledge. Now little did I know, I was being catfished. And I even asked God, because I didn't hear from J in a few days, "Lord, if I'm going to marry this man, please have him call me right now."

Well, all of a sudden, he called. Now J was husband number 5. But because I was being catfished, I became desperate. A man named N became interested in me on the same site and even paid my way, and with some other people from the website, to come visit in Kentucky. I was excited. My first vacation. Now, online, I would joke around with a friend of mine named Fish. And we'd joke around from zombies to pumpkin cheesecake. And everyone, if they want to, can listen to your comments to one another if you want to share them. Well, N had made me a pumpkin cheesecake, and I saw it in the fridge. It was a surprise for me. And I was so captivated by how he had made it for me because he spoke a love language of mine. So I chose to date him. He would send me flowers, and he wanted to marry me, and I did too. I loved how he would play his acoustic guitar, and I'd sing to it. Well, when we got married, probably not even two months later, things went bad, and I mean quick. I found out he was going to prostitutes. He asked me to put my children in boarding school. We started to fight physically. I was dealing with sickness at the time, and he'd tell me that all I was, was a debt to him. That it was because of me that he paid taxes to support people like me on welfare. I remember that I was reading in Job, and I was balding on top of my head, and out loud I remember rebuking Satan, and I told him, "If you want my hair, take it, I can buy a wig at Walmart." It was interesting because I was worried, but when God showed me, in the book of Job, what Satan said, I knew what he was up to. Job 2:4: "Skin for skin! A man will give all he has for his own life."

I don't know why, but that gave me hope and trust in God. During this time, I had many demonic attacks. I had heard of a guy on the Christian website talk about an incubus. I laughed so hard at this guy because I was like, "There is no way demons would be having sex with people." Well, lo and behold, I woke up in the morning, and I had woken up because I felt someone humping me. My husband at this point was no longer making love to me. He was going away on the weekends and wouldn't tell me where and that it wasn't any of my business. I had woken up, and nothing was there, but it felt like my soul was being sucked out of me. I remembered the guy saying to say the name of Jesus. So I did, tried to at least, to reach toward my Bible, and immediately it was gone. I called my mom and told her what had happened, and she said, "You know, Christina, I just spoke to a friend about that, and I wondered why God had brought that up, and now I know, it was for this conversation."

I had another attack. Out of the blue, my head started pounding, like a really bad migraine. Not a headache. I can have migraines for up to three days just by not having caffeine, and my sight is impacted, etc. I knew this wasn't normal, and I yelled out, "Satan, I know what you're doing! Be gone in Jesus's name! You have no authority over my body!" Immediately the pain was gone.

My marriage did not last more than a couple of months. My children even watched this man push me into the glass shower doors because I was taking a shower and stepped out to dry off, and he was angry with me and pushed me. And my baby brother was there, and my husband was upset because how could I have him in our house when he's not even a Christian. It was Christmastime, and I wanted to spend it with him, but my brother chose to leave after my husband had kicked him out of the house. I asked my husband how could he do this. My brother had flown up here to see me, and now he's out in the snow with no place to go. My husband ended up having him come back to the house and gave him one hundred dollars. That night, I bought some liquor and drank till I blacked out.

After my brother left, N was arrested for more abuse, and of course, I pleaded for the judge to forgive, and we'd work it out. And I remember getting home, and my husband completely hated me. I had never felt so much hate from a person, especially when they say that they are a Christian.

About a couple of weeks later, I called the women's abuse shelter for a place to stay because I could no longer allow my children to see what was going on. I was in fear for my life, especially when the police said that he'd seen women in body bags being carried out of their homes from their husbands abusing them to where it ended up in him killing her, even when he didn't mean to.

I had contacted my daughter's father, J, about what was going on. I decided to go to Naples. I wanted to be with the man that I thought God wanted me to be with because he was in Miami. I started talking to him online again, and the same thing was happening. He'd reel me in and then throw the fishing line back out again. It took about a month, but the women's homeless shelter in Naples became open for us four. Getting one bed is hard, but four beds is very hard. I was looking at a four- to six-month wait. When it became open, I drove down from Kentucky to Florida.

Being in the divorce process, I needed to get an attorney because my husband had gotten one. It was messy and painful. Now being at the shelter, God opened doors. And I made mistakes, stupid mistakes. I had my schooling paid for while I was down there. I did school and worked one to two jobs at the time. Learned more about people being lost. And I started to grow more in Christ, with stupid mistakes. I won't get into all of that, but one thing I do want to show here that had happened. I had gotten a Facebook message from the sister of my son's father while I was in the shelter. What had happened was, a tree branch fell from eighty feet and snapped his spine in half. I've only had a few times in my life where I have mourned, and this was one of those times. I told the homeless shelter about it, and I told them I was going whether I got permission or not. And if they were going to kick me out, then so be it. But the Lord was watching over, and I didn't get kicked out. I went to Connecticut and visited T. With what I am about to show you, it's all Christ. This is how much Christ loves T. He laid it on my heart to buy this man who was in the hospital, with no one visiting him, clothes, shoes, food, and some items for entertainment. I got to share the love of Christ with him, and he still rejected Him. T would tell me, "You've changed, there's something different about you." I'd let him know that it was Jesus. This was the same man who destroyed all my mother's things that I was given, my grandma's letters to me, my baby pictures, and the only picture I have of my mom, but Jesus still loves this man, to where when I got back to Florida, he put on my heart to stop and forgive his child support debt, which was over ten thousand dollars. And I obeyed with gladness in my heart. That's the love of Christ. It doesn't matter what he does, as long as he comes home (to Christ). That's the love that we should have for every person, including our enemies.

Now onto husband number 4. That was Lily's father, J. I thought it was the right thing to do, plus I still had love in my heart for him. But that was short. Same situation but a different face. We had been both abusive to each other before when we were together and now in this marriage. At one point, my son, who was six at the time, stepped in front of me and told J that he wasn't going to hurt his mommy. You know, during these different marriages, not one time did I seek God, with what He wanted. I came up with the idea and then went with it. Because you know, I know the Word better than God, right? Of course not. During this time, I ended up going very legalistic. No pork, honoring all feasts with no exceptions, and all of my Sabbaths needed without a doubt to be holy. This was about two years now since I got saved; I was searching for the right denomination. In all honesty, I learned that it became my form of control. I had a lot of hurt. I was trying to keep over six hundred plus laws from the Bible. Why I am bringing this up is because it is important.

During this time, even though I did not seek God for answers, I want to share my Christian growth as well. We all see backsliding in this. I started to become angry with people who did not want to keep God's commandments. At this time, my brother London had been making some bad choices. One night in a dream, I saw him driving fast and running his car off this bridge area that had a metal rail along it. Immediately I woke up, and I started to pray for my brother for safety. At this time, London wasn't talking to any of the family, but when we did talk, he had let me know that he had gotten into a car crash, and if it wasn't for the metal rail, his car would have flown off the bridge. I immediately told him that I had a dream about that and woke up and started praying for him for his safety. It still didn't faze him.

Probably about some months later, my brother got involved again in heroin, but this time, the consequences took his life. It was a two-month battle of going from hospital to hospital, having five surgeries where his intestines just fell apart because he had Ehlers-Danlos syndrome (EDS). I was working ninety hours a week and then traveling a little over an hour to be with him at the hospital. My husband was saying some hurtful things, asking me how I was enjoying my vacation away from my kids. There were times that I couldn't even talk because I was so hurt. My baby brother, who I met just at sixteen, now was going to be taken away. Another one whom I love. He ended up being sent home. He had a mesh, and the hospital didn't even give him anything for the mesh, and we had to rig things to get the fluids out from overflowing all over his body. At this point, he was a skeleton. All bones. He couldn't speak, but I read to him about the prodigal son in the Bible.

Luke 15:11–32

And he said, "There was a man who had two sons. 12 And the younger of them said to his father, 'Father, give me the share of property that is coming to me.' And he divided his property between them. 13 Not many days later, the younger son gathered all he had and took a journey into a far country, and there he squandered his property in reckless living. 14 And when he had spent everything, a severe famine arose in that country, and he began to be in need. 15 So he went and hired himself out to[a] one of the citizens of that country, who sent him into his fields to feed pigs. 16 And he was longing to be fed with the pods that the pigs ate, and no one gave him anything.

17 "But when he came to himself, he said, 'How many of my father's hired servants have more than enough bread, but I perish here with hunger! 18 I will arise and go to my father, and I will say to him, "Father, I have sinned against heaven and before you. 19 I am no longer worthy to be called your son. Treat me as one of your hired servants."' 20 And he arose and came to his father. But while he was still a long way off, his father saw him and felt compassion, and ran and embraced him and kissed him. 21 And the son said to him, 'Father, I have sinned against heaven and before you. I am no longer worthy to be called your son.' 22 But the father said to his servants, 'Bring quickly the best robe, and put it on him, and put a ring on his hand, and shoes on his feet. 23 And bring the fattened calf and kill it, and let us eat and celebrate. 24 For this my son was dead, and is alive again; he was lost, and is found.' And they began to celebrate.

25 "Now his older son was in the field, and as he came and drew near to the house, he heard music

and dancing. 26 And he called one of the servants and asked what these things meant. 27 And he said to him, 'Your brother has come, and your father has killed the fattened calf, because he has received him back safe and sound.' 28 But he was angry and refused to go in. His father came out and entreated him, 29 but he answered his father, 'Look, these many years I have served you, and I never disobeyed your command, yet you never gave me a young goat, that I might celebrate with my friends. 30 But when this son of yours came, who has devoured your property with prostitutes, you killed the fattened calf for him!' 31 And he said to him, 'Son, you are always with me, and all that is mine is yours. 32 It was fitting to celebrate and be glad, for this your brother was dead, and is alive; he was lost, and is found.'"

That was one of the last things that I read and said to him because I remember telling him after reading that, "London, it doesn't matter what you have done, as long as you come home." My aunt T did say that when he was able to talk, he did accept Jesus into his heart as his savior. I hope that is true.

At Christmastime, which I stopped celebrating because it is derived from pagan traditions, I saw this old man dressed like Santa at this small mom-and-pop breakfast place. I was upset, not only because he was dressed up like Santa, but then passing out stuffed animals. "How wicked and evil is that?" I told my husband. But when I saw that old man handing one to my child and how he reached out to give it to my child, his hand was shaking, like he had Parkinson's disease. Immediately, I went to the bathroom and bawled my eyes out. I said, "Forgive me, Lord, this man is showing more love by doing what he is doing than I. All I am doing is condemning this man." I remember telling a loved one of mine what had happened, and they told me that I was in the wrong for feeling the way I did. I came to the conclusion that night that I will have God lead me in the Word and not man, no matter how close I am to them. I had to get all I was taught from man out of my head and go to God to relearn His Word. And what it means to live for Him.

My marriage to J had ended, and during my pain, that just kept being stacked like pancakes. By this time, I probably had a whole house of pancakes plus some, I reconnected with J from the chat site. I tried to keep my fourth marriage, but drugs and alcohol had been more important. People cannot be unequally yoked. I started talking, and this was the time that we finally got to meet. We met after I had given him five hundred in donations and ten thousand in my bank. He saw that from the last time we spoke, I had furthered my career and was making really good money. I got to listen to him teach the Bible on the computer, and I loved that. All I wanted was a godly man, with whom I could go into ministry together. But little did I know, it was all a front.

After my fourth divorce, I would travel to Naples to meet with J. And of course, we had intimacy at a hotel, and we looked at that as marriage.

Well, I have to admit, I was so biblically inaccurate. Surprise, surprise. I also idolized this man. I didn't realize it at first, but this man was my idol. I had moved to the hotel with my kids until we could get a place together, but plans changed. He had to move in with me because he ended up having his boys full-time all of a sudden because his ex-wife had abused her eight-year-old son. She beat him with a shoe to where his back was black and blue with welts all over it. So all three children had to go with their dads. Before I get too much into this situation with husband number 5, Jesus also died and loves both these people. This lady, N, has a lot of hurt in her life. I'm not saying what she has done and does is right; sin is the cause of all this pain, not only to her, but to others around her as well. And to give some background to J, his mother was drunk one day, and she climbed up a crane (which she did many times). She either slipped and fell off of it by accident or on purpose, but either way, was found dead, and a son, J, was hurt from it.

So when I tell you about this marriage number 5, because it's really bad and the most damaging marriage that I have ever been in, understand that Jesus still loves this man, and it doesn't matter what he has done or is doing now. Jesus just wants him to come to Him (salvation). Please understand that I am in no way stating that sin is not a big deal. It is because Jesus paid that price for us. One sin is death. What I am saying is that we need not focus on a person's sin, but their heart because of course, they will have sin problems. No surprise there. When they get saved, they will not want to sin, and they will start to be sanctified by Christ. To me, sin is the distraction; it's the person's heart that matters.

This is the last marriage I will be sharing. I have been avoiding this one especially because this one has hurt the most. Due to my sin of idolizing this man, God gave me over to my idol. Of course, we know where that ends: in death. I had been obsessed with this man. I was stuck on the idea that "this is the man that God has for me to marry." I don't know if God facepalms, but right now, I'm facepalming. I put God to the side. I wanted my cake and my ice cream too. I can't help but laugh right now because how many times did it take to get hurt over and over again to finally trust God? I ended up finding this man online again, and when I did, we started to converse. He was leading Bible studies online, and I'd donate money to him, sometimes five hundred dollars. He constantly needed help with things, and of course, I wanted to be his hero, or in his eyes, sugar mama. Little did I know, the same attention he gave to me, he, too, was giving to other women, whether old or young. He had seen that through the years I had gone from a home health aide to a CNA, and I told him how much money I made, which in his eyes was a good amount. So with that, we met. And the first night we met, we had known each other that night. We were now married. Even with me being in sin, God did teach me something that night about the longing desire for the bridegroom and the ten virgins. God still showing me that I should long for Him that way, not a man. Now that I look back, I see that, but during that time, everything was about J because I wanted it to be.

He would ask me to do errands for his ex-wife, which I would. I did not realize that he and her were still a thing. At this time, I had gotten a hotel with my children until J and I could get a rental together, but due to her having beat her youngest son, all of a sudden, I had J's sons and J with us in this small hotel room. I worked 110 hours a week trying to get us into a place. We finally did get into a place and then shortly after J's ex-wife had completed the things that she needed to do to get her children back, we then had a DCF call in our life. She told the state that I was molesting her children at the time that she didn't have them (about three months). That is what destroyed me. I was never home, I left my work (live-in caregiver) at the time just to talk to the DCF worker, and when I did see my kids, I was running from one client to the next, I'd drop by their school just to give them a kiss. That night, I had recorded the teenage boys because while my husband was talking to the DCF worker outside, they were bragging about how they lied to the DCF worker because their mom felt threatened that I had mentioned that she shouldn't claim the boys on her taxes but ours, a conversation that they had heard between their dad and me. And the boys had let me know that if I was going to hurt their mom in any way that this stuff would continue to happen. I showed the DCF worker what I had recorded, to protect me and my children. Even though these boys were very abusive to my children and me, they didn't all of a sudden become this way because I was in the picture. They had problems before that. This did bring out a lot of their problems, but one thing I tell my children when they start to talk about the pain from this past, I tell them to pray for them.

That night, I wanted to die. I just layed in my bed all night, lifeless. The next morning, I went to a counselor and told her that the thought of dying came to my mind by drinking until I didn't wake up anymore. People didn't understand that this DCF call that the mother had made reminded me of my past rape at four and ongoing. Not only would I relive it, but I could feel being raped again and again. And every time I saw the boys, it would then trigger because I'd remember what their mom did.

The counselor, after hearing what was going on, told me that I was in an abusive marriage. Of course, I'd give excuses. I'm married now, and it's too late. I also wanted to make it work. I didn't want to give up. Things kept getting worse. My husband, who said that he had left drugs when he got saved, visited his dad with me and started to do drugs again and asked me to do it with him. I could tell that God was saying, "No," but I said, "Yes."

The drugs, on top of the lies, made things worse. I remember the first time; it was at night. I had very little time at home, only a few hours, and he'd leave the house trashed. So I needed to get it up to par. I asked him to move his weight bench out of the kitchen, and he said no. I started to move the bench, and he (320 pounds) ran up to it and sat on it, hurting my foot because it was under it, and I screamed in pain. Then we started yelling at each other (in front of the kids), and he threw my juicer at me and the glass coffeepot my mom got me. So I took his phone, and because I couldn't break it, I then peed on it. All I could do was cry. The boys thought it was hysterical. But that night, all that was talked about was my behavior and my peeing on the phone.

When we got officially married, which by this time we are, J had done it because he was in seminary school about to graduate in a year, and his boss, who was the principal of the Christian school he worked at, told him that we needed to be married. I put this in there because when my uncle, who's a pastor, and we'd get marriage counseling from him and my aunt, he pointed out something that I never even thought of. He had asked, "Did you guys pray together before getting married to see if this was the right thing to do?" We both looked at each other, and I was like, "Ommoo," in my head, of course.

So our marriage became destructive, and it was so bad that when summertime rolled around, he was out of a job. He didn't like the position that he wanted and was on drugs and didn't see that his aggression was getting so bad. He even told off the principal (his boss) at the school, and they issued a no-trespassing order against him. So I needed more hours; my client had passed, and my other one I could no longer do because my PTSD was so bad that I could no longer be a live-in care provider anymore. I want to give you an example of how bad my PTSD was. I was sleeping, literally, and I am having a dream. I had a dream that J's son was suffocating my son in the bedroom, and I run into the kitchen, and my dream turns from dream to reality because I saw in my dream J's son suffocating my son. As I got in the kitchen, the dream faded away. So in a way, I ran while sleeping to the kitchen, you could say. When I got to the kitchen, I burst out in tears and repeated to myself, "It was only a dream, he is not in there suffocating my son." So I went in there, everything was fine, and I put some covers over J's son because it was cold, we didn't have heat in the house, and I went off to bed.

I ended up going 4 hours away for work, the same 110 hours a week. If I got at least a 10-hour period together, I'd drive down 4 hours, stay 2 hours, and drive back up 4 hours. I was doing this for about 3 months.

We had cameras in our house that J wanted. Many times, though, they were shut off. And one time I had so much anxiety over what he was doing, I called for a welfare checkup. He would say nasty things and hang up on me when I asked him to turn back on the cameras so I could see that my kids were okay. Come to find out now, he would leave my kids home a lot; they were six, seven, and eight, and he had watched porn in front of my seven-year-old daughter from time to time. They also told me that he wouldn't feed them and that my one bunny he shot with a pellet gun for fun and killed it. I didn't know any of this until we were homeless, not even a year later from then.

I remember during the three months, I would stay with my aunt, who is a witch. And I remember being in the room I was in, I cried out to God. I asked Him, "Why did You leave me?"

I heard Him say, "I didn't leave, you did." I apologized to God. And I wanted to make changes.

After three months, I could no longer work. I was then being physically abused. He was arrested at one point, but I dropped it. He wrote up a paper for the state attorney for me to give them, and they dropped the charges. I was thrown into a wall, to where I got stuck in it.

During this time, we were making videos for Jesus. J was in the nursing home ministry, and that stopped when I told my aunt that he was doing drugs. I told my husband that if he didn't stop within a week, I'd let them know because he shouldn't be doing ministry if he's getting high every day. Well, this led him to hate me completely now. I kept going to counseling, and they wanted to put me on Zoloft. I refused; I knew that my environment needed to change. I was praying for J to be led by the Lord. Now I had made a lot of money, and about everything we had, I paid for. The phones, tablets, clothes, etc. And I had gone from smashing these things to where I would then walk away and pray. I had smashed the phones and tablets because again I found porn. I even wondered at times about a relationship between him and a seventh grader. He had about twenty pictures on his computer of her, her cell number, and then her birth-date in his Google calendar. When I'd confront him on this, because that was one of his class students, he'd hurt me and tell me that I had a sick mind.

There was a lot of mental abuse. I got to the point, I could only sit on a chair, staring out the window all day. I was also drinking at this point. DCF was involved over and over again. One of J's boys, every time he'd pass me in the house, would come up to me and almost punch me to where his fists would be on top of my nose, and he would laugh. That would then trigger the event that happened when I was seventeen, getting beaten with a dog training collar. J's son was also physically abusing my children and would make excuses for it. My husband never stood up for me or my children. He was always protective of his ex-wife. I saw her leaving our home at night when I had been away for three months, working.

We then went through an eviction, he said he wanted us to move out of state. I thought this would be the light at the end of the tunnel. We packed what we had in the car and made a stop first at my aunt's. We were trying to get donations from people because the ministry was going to tell others about Christ. Well, this all was a lie. And if a "Christian's" lifestyle is like this anyway, they shouldn't be in ministry because all it's doing is giving Jesus a bad name.

My husband ended up dropping us off at a hotel six hours away from where we were, took everything and the car, and went down to live with his ex-wife and children. They still managed to call DCF for one last time, in hopes of getting my children taken away. (My husband told me that over the phone.)

I remember the DCF worker asking me, "What do you hate most about parenting?" I had told her, "I hate seeing the mistakes that I have made affect my children."

That first week, I felt life come back to me. The demonic activity stopped, the suicidal thoughts, the feeling of being lifeless. It was like a black sheet was gone from over my head. I had started to believe the same doctrine that my husband believed, which was insane, and I am not even going to mention what it was, but now believing in the Holy Spirit, I was allowing Him to lead me again.

During this time, there was a lot of pain that my children had told me and that they needed to heal from. I made my daughter a promise that I would not work over sixty hours a week. That I would raise them and not someone else, and I started to pray with them at night and teach them the Word of God.

I was so selfish, I wanted leadership, but at whose expense? My kids. I thought to myself, *I can do both.* One thing for a long time that I didn't believe was that your children are the biggest ministry that a person will ever have. And it is. God has shown me so much mercy and grace. His hand has not left our home. He provides left and right. He is our protector, and He is our provider. For a long time, it's been hard for me to trust people, but more so God. I hate it. Why do I have such a hard time with being still and knowing that God is God? Why do I have such a hard time understanding why God loves me? It's because He is loving. Our home still at times is under attack, but we have God. This is why I wrote this book. That even though I've made so many poor decisions, He still loves me. And He loves you too.

For the fact that one day we will all be held accountable for every sin that we have committed, for every word that has come out of our mouth and every thought that we have ever had. Jesus, knowing how much He is and would be hated, still died for someone like me and everyone here on earth. He went through the torture of being beaten and humiliated to where people couldn't even recognize His face because of how badly He was beaten for us. He was also whipped forty times. The movie *The Passion of the Christ* doesn't do it justice. And on top of being beaten and then nailed to a cross, He thinks of His mother, for His disciple John to take care of her. He thinks of the thief on his side and the men who have beaten Him, asking the Lord, His Father, to forgive them. He always thought of people, including His enemies. All because He knows what will happen in the future. We all have to take accountability for our actions. And He paid the price for that. There is a heaven and a hell, whether we agree with it or not. Jesus doesn't want anyone to perish. He has given us free will though. The way to heaven is through Jesus. We can either say yes or say no. He won't ever force Himself on anyone. I am a perfect example. I chose many wrong ways, which has caused pain not only to me but to my children and even those around me. This is how beautiful God is; He shows us mercy when we don't deserve it. He's waiting for us to give Him our hearts. That's all He wants.

John 4:1–42

Now when Jesus learned that the Pharisees had heard that Jesus was making and baptizing more disciples than John 2 (although Jesus himself did not baptize, but only his disciples), 3 he left Judea and departed again for Galilee. 4 And he had to pass through Samaria. 5 So he came to a town of Samaria called Sychar, near the field that Jacob had given to his son Joseph. 6 Jacob's well was there; so Jesus, wearied as he was from his journey, was sitting beside the well. It was about the sixth hour.

7 A woman from Samaria came to draw water. Jesus said to her, "Give me a drink." 8 (For his disciples had gone away into the city to buy food.) 9 The Samaritan woman said to him, "How is it that you, a

Jew, ask for a drink from me, a woman of Samaria?" (For Jews have no dealings with Samaritans.) 10 Jesus answered her, "If you knew the gift of God, and who it is that is saying to you, 'Give me a drink,' you would have asked him, and he would have given you living water." 11 The woman said to him, "Sir, you have nothing to draw water with, and the well is deep. Where do you get that living water? 12 Are you greater than our father Jacob? He gave us the well and drank from it himself, as did his sons and his livestock." 13 Jesus said to her, "Everyone who drinks of this water will be thirsty again, 14 but whoever drinks of the water that I will give him will never be thirsty again. The water that I will give him will become in him a spring of water welling up to eternal life." 15 The woman said to him, "Sir, give me this water, so that I will not be thirsty or have to come here to draw water."

16 Jesus said to her, "Go, call your husband, and come here." 17 The woman answered him, "I have no husband." Jesus said to her, "You are right in saying, 'I have no husband'; 18 for you have had five husbands, and the one you now have is not your husband. What you have said is true." 19 The woman said to him, "Sir, I perceive that you are a prophet. 20 Our fathers worshiped on this mountain, but you say that in Jerusalem is the place where people ought to worship." 21 Jesus said to her, "Woman, believe me, the hour is coming when neither on this mountain nor in Jerusalem will you worship the Father. 22 You worship what you do not know; we worship what we

know, for salvation is from the Jews. 23 But the hour is coming, and is now here, when the true worshipers will worship the Father in spirit and truth, for the Father is seeking such people to worship him. 24 God is spirit, and those who worship him must worship in spirit and truth." 25 The woman said to him, "I know that Messiah is coming (he who is called Christ). When he comes, he will tell us all things." 26 Jesus said to her, "I who speak to you am he."

27 Just then his disciples came back. They marveled that he was talking with a woman, but no one said, "What do you seek?" or, "Why are you talking with her?" 28 So the woman left her water jar and went away into town and said to the people, 29 "Come, see a man who told me all that I ever did. Can this be the Christ?" 30 They went out of the town and were coming to him.

31 Meanwhile the disciples were urging him, saying, "Rabbi, eat." 32 But he said to them, "I have food to eat that you do not know about." 33 So the disciples said to one another, "Has anyone brought him something to eat?" 34 Jesus said to them, "My food is to do the will of him who sent me and to accomplish his work. 35 Do you not say, 'There are yet four months, then comes the harvest'? Look, I tell you, lift up your eyes, and see that the fields are white for harvest. 36 Already the one who reaps is receiving wages and gathering fruit for eternal life, so that sower and reaper may rejoice together. 37 For here the saying holds true, 'One sows and another reaps.' 38 I sent you to reap that for which you did

not labor. Others have labored, and you have entered into their labor."

39 Many Samaritans from that town believed in him because of the woman's testimony, "He told me all that I ever did." 40 So when the Samaritans came to him, they asked him to stay with them, and he stayed there two days. 41 And many more believed because of his word. 42 They said to the woman, "It is no longer because of what you said that we believe, for we have heard for ourselves, and we know that this is indeed the Savior of the world."

About the Author

I was a broken individual, saved by Christ. Since I have been a new creation in Him, I am a loving mother and wife. I care for the needy and try to be like Christ every day that I am here on earth.

www.ingramcontent.com/pod-product-compliance
Lightning Source LLC
Chambersburg PA
CBHW031413160726
47993CB00003B/1218